RIGI

(READ IT GRASP IT)

ETYMOLOGY

The Study of Words' Origin

Vocabulary Book for students from Class 5th to Post Graduation

Also Suitable for
GRE, CAT, GMAT, UPSC, State PSC, Bank PO, SSC, SAT, XAT, MAT, IELTS, TOEFL, SNAP, IBSAT, Aptitude test of public Sector unit like SAIL, GAIL, NFL, ONGC exams etc. & for all English Learner

Umesh Sehgal

RIGI PUBLICATION
777, STREET NO 9, KRISHNA NAGAR, KHANNA-141401 (PUNJAB), INDIA
Phone: +91-9357710014, +91-9465468291
Website: www.rigipublication.com
Email: info@rigipublication.com

RIGI ETYMOLOGY
The Study of Words' Origin
Umesh Sehgal

2nd Edition

©copyright 2013 by RIGI PUBLICATION

Prior edition ©copyright 2009 by RIGI PUBLICATION

Originally published in the India

ISBN: 978-81-907513-1-5

Published by RIGI PUBLICATION
777, Street no.9, Krishna Nagar
Khanna-141401 (Punjab)
Website: www.rigipublication.com
Email: info@rigipublication.com
Phone: +91-9357710014, +91-9465468291

Printed at Aarna Printing Solutions, Patiala

Dedication

*Dedicated to all vocabulary
hunting students with inspiration to
solve their problems of learning
from the roots of words.*

# Root of Words' Origin

INTRODUCTION

Every effort is made to make the book easily understandable. Rigi Etymology bears no resemblance to any other English vocabulary book. The Book contains two parts. First part has roots of origin of words of different objects & the second part has words denoting nature, animals, marriages, professions etc. This book is very beautiful combination of vocabulary to be learned in a very easy way. It will satisfy the hunger of students trying to learn vocabulary. It will improve your English enormously & will give you deep knowledge of words by linking words and by prefixes & suffixes. It is a treasure of words with their meanings to clear any competitive exams like GRE, CAT, GMAT, UPSC, State PSC, Bank PO, SSC, SAT, XAT, MAT, IELTS, TOEFL, SNAP, IBSAT, Aptitude test of public Sector unit like SAIL, GAIL, NFL, ONGC exams etc.

It is hoped that the book will be found useful for one and all especially those for whom it is meant.

Comments and suggestions are most welcomed.

"Man is made by his belief. As he believes, so he is."

For comments & suggestions please go to our website:

www.rigipublication.com

With Best Wishes
Umesh Sehgal
Author

<u>**Contents**</u>   <u>**Sr. No.**</u>

PART - 1

ROOTS OF WORDS

1. Ambi	**:On both sides**
Ambivert	: Person having balance between introversion and extroversion
Ambiguity	: Double meaning
Ambivalent	: The co-existence of opposite feelings in one (e.g. Love and hate)
Ambidextrous	: Able to use left and right hands equally
2. Anti	**: Opposed to**
Antipathy	: Dislike or feeling of aversion
Antipyretic	: Something that reduces fever
Antihero	: The protagonist who lacks traditional heroic qualities
Antidote	: Medicine given to counteract poison
Anticlockwise	: Opposite in movement to the movement of the hands of a clock
3. Arch	**: Principal, Chief, ruler, leader**
Archetype	: A prototype
Archangel	: A chief angel
Archbishop	: A bishop at the head of an ecclesiastical province

4. Astra : **Related to stars**

Astronaut : Space traveller

Astrophysics : Branch of astronomy concerned with the physics and chemistry of heavenly bodies

Astral : Connected with or consisting of stars

Asterisk : Star-shaped symbol used to mark words etc, for reference or distinction

Astrology : Art of judging reputed occult influence of stars, planets etc. on human affairs.

Asterism : Cluster of stars

Astrolabe : Instrument for measuring altitudes of stars etc.

5. Anthropos : **Man Kind**

Anthropometry : Study of Measurement of the human body.

Anthropoid : Humanoid or Resembling a human, especially in shape or outward appearance.

Anthropographic : Branch of anthropology dealing with geographic distribution of human beings.

Anthropogenesis	: The study of the origin and development of human beings.
Anthropomorphism	: Attribution of human form to god, animal etc.
Anthropocentric	: Considering man as central fact of the universe
Anthropophagy	: The eating of human flesh; cannibalism.
Anthropology	: Study of mankind
Misanthrope	: One who hates mankind
Philanthropist	: Lover of mankind

6. -age **: Collection or action**

Haulage	: The act of pulling
Peerage	: The rank of peer
Bondage	: The state of serfdom or slavery
Baggage	: Collection of items of luggage
Acreage	: Area in acres
Breakage	Act of breaking, loss by breaking

7. –accous **: Consisting of**

Farinaceous	: Starchy
Argillaceous	: Containing clay, having the characteristics of clay
Herbaceous	: Having the characteristics of a herb
Tuffaceous	: Having the characteristics features of rock composed of volcanic ash

8. -ate **: To cause, to make**

Emancipate	: To set free from control
Arrogate	: To claim as one's own without right
Deviate	: Cause to stray
Consecrate	: To make sacred
Decimate	: To destroy large numbers
Infiltrate	: To cause to slip through
Segregate	: To keep apart
Enervate	: To take away strength

9. Ante **: Before**

Antenatal	: Occurring previous to birth
Antedate	: Affix an earlier date
Antecedent	: Previous, prior in time or order

| Antediluvian | : antiquated, Of the period before the flood, utterly out of date |

10. Bio — **: Living**

Biopsy	: Examination of a living tissue
Biography	: Written life of a person
Biology	: Science of life
Biogenic	: Produced by living organisms
Biota	: The flora and fauna of a region
Biosis	: Mode of life
Autobiography	: Writing the story of one's own life
Biosphere	: Part of the world in which life exists

11. Bene — **: Good, well**

Benediction	: A blessing
Benevolent	: Disposed to do good
Benefactor	: A person who does good
Beneficent	: Performing acts of kindness and charity
Benefit	: Something which promotes well-being

12. Bi   **: Twice, doubly**

Bilingual   : Able to speak two languages with ease

Biannual   : Occurring twice a year

Bicameral   : Consisting of two legislative chambers

Bigamy   : The act of being married a second time while previous marriage is still in existence.

Bilateral   : Binding two parties

13. -cide   **: Killing**

Fratricide   : The killing of one's brother

Autocide   : The killing of self and others in an automotive vehicle

Matricide   : The killing of one's mother

Uxoricide   : The killing of one's wife

Sororicide   : The killing of one's sister

Patricide   : The killing of one's father

Genocide   : The killing of race

Infanticide   : The killing of infants

| Homicide | : The killing of human being |
| Suicide | : The killing of oneself |

14. Circum : **Around on all sides**

Circumvent	: A surrounding condition
Circumstance	: A surrounding condition
Circumscribe	: To draw a line around something
Circumnavigate	: To sail around something
Circumambulate	: To walk around an object as part of a religious ritual
Circumference	: The boundary line of a circle or any closed curve
Circumlocution	: A roundabout way of saving something

15. Contra : **Against, Contrary**

Counterstatement	: A statement denying another statement
Contravene	: To come or be in conflict with
Countermand	: To order in opposition to an order previously given thereby annulling it.
Counterbalance	: To oppose something with equal

force

Contraband	: Articles brought into the country against the law
Contradict	: To say the opposite

16. Calor   **: Heat**

Caloricity	: Ability to develop and maintain animal heat
Calorie	: A unit of heat
Calorimeter	: Instrument for measuring the quantity of heat
Cauldron	: A huge vessel for boiling
Calorescence	: Heat waves changed to light

17. -cian   **: Having a skill or art**

Beautician	: An expert in beauty care
Mortician	: An undertaker
Dietician	: An expert in food and nutrition
Pediatrician	: A doctor whose specialty is care of children
Obstetrician	: A doctor whose specialty is delivering babies

18. Chronos   : **Time**

Chronic   : Marked by long duration or frequent recurrence

Chronology   : The science that deals with the determination of dates and the sequence of events.

Chronometer   : An instrument for measuring time

Chronograph   : An instrument for accurately measuring and recording time intervals

Chronometry   : Accurate time measurement

19. Cephal   : **Head**

Encephalitis   : inflammation of the brain

Megacephalic   : Large headed

Cephalothorax   : the united head and thorax of an arachnid or higher crustacean

Cephalic   : Of or relating to the head

20. -cise   : **Cut**

Excision   : The cutting out, removing of

Precise   : Cut right, cut with precision

Concise   : Cut short

Incise

: Cut into, as incise an abscess or infection

21. Dorm

: Sleep

Dormitory

: A large bedroom for a number of people in a school or institution.

Dormitive

: Causing sleep, as a drug or sleeping portion

Dormancy

: State of being static, motionless

Dormant

: (of an animal) Having normal physical functions suspended or slowed down for a period of time; in or as if in a deep sleep.
(of a plant or bud) Alive but not actively growing.

22. Dia

: Through or Across

Diatribe

: A long and bitter discussion which is usually abusive

Dialectic

: Argument through critical discussion

Diameter

: The length of a line drawn through the centre of the circle

Diadermal

: Acting through the skin

Diagnose

: Recognize a disease through symptoms

| Diagonal | : Passing through two opposite angles of a plane figure |

23. Dys : **bad or Mal**

Dyscrasia	: An abnormal condition of the body or one of its parts
Dysphoria	: State of unease or mental discomfort
Dyslexia	: A general term for disorders that involve difficulty in learning to read or interpret words, letters, and other symbols, but that do not affect general intelligence
Dysfunction	: Impaired or abnormal functioning

24. Dem and Demo : **People**

Demotist	: A student of sociological writings
Demography	: Study of populations, births and deaths
Democracy	: Government of the people
Demagogue	: A leader who exploits the weaknesses of the mob

25. -ectomy : **Surgical removal**

| Gastrectomy | : Surgical removal of an ulcer |

| Hysterectomy | : Surgical removal of the uterus |

26. Epi : **at besides, over upon**

Epicenter	: The part of the earth's surface directly above the place of origin of an earthquake
Epicontinental	: Lying on continent or continental shelf
Epiblast	: The outer layer of an embryo at a very early stage in its development
Epigastric	: Living on or over the stomach

27. -ee : **One who**

Donee	: One who receives a gift
Deportee	: One who is deported
Nominee	: One who is nominated
Collate	: One on whom a benefice is bestowed
Absentee	: One who is absent

28. Equi : **Equal**

| Equiangular | : Having all or corresponding angles equal |
| Equivocal | : Subject to two or more |

interpretations

Equilibrium	: A state of balance, a state of intellectual or emotional balance
Equidistant	: Equally distant
Equipoise	: A state of equilibrium, a counter balance
Equipollent	: Equal in force, power, validity or effect
Equilateral	: Having all sides equal
Equilibrate	: To bring into equilibrium, balance
Equivalent	: Equal in force, amount or value

29. Ecto   **: Outside**

Ectoderm	: Outermost layer of embryo in early development
Ectoparasite	: A parasite that lives on the exterior of its host
Ectogenous	: Capable of development apart from the host
Ectoplasm	: The outer layer of the cytoplasm of a cell
Ectozoom	: External parasite

30. Ego   **: Self**

Egotist   : One who has self-conceit

Ego trip   : An act, experience, or course of behaviour that gratifies the ego.

Egotism   : The practice of talking about oneself too much

Egocentric   : limited in outlook or concern to one's own activities or needs or being self-centered or selfish

Egomania   : One who is morbidly obsessed with oneself

Egoist   : Selfish person

Alter ego   : One's other self

31. Ex- (e or ef)   **: Out, out of, of from, thoroughly, completely**

Exclude   :To shut out

Exterminate   : To wipe out

Effervesce   : To give out bubbles of gas

Exhume   : To dig out of ground

Excavate   : To hollow out of the earth

Exhale   : To breathe out

Exfoliate	: To come off in layers

32. Eco : **Concerned with the interrelationship of living organism and their environments**

Ecosphere	: The parts of the universe habitable by living organism
Ecospecies	: A taxonomic species regarded as an ecological unit
Ecosystem	: System of interacting organisms in a particular habitat

33. Forth : **Onwards**

Forthcoming	: Approaching
Forthright	: Going straight to the point without ambiguity
Forthwith	: Immediately

34. Flec and flex : **To bend**

Flexible	: Able to bend
Flexuous	: Having many bends
Genuflect	: Bend the knee esp. in worship
Flexor	: A muscle which serves to bend a limb

| Flection | : Bending, curvature, bent state |

35. Forte : **Strong**

Forte	: One's strong point
Fortification	: A stronghold
Force	: Power, strength
Fortitude	: Strength of mind and character to endure
Fortress	: A fortified Place

36. Geronto : **Old age or Old person**

| Gerontocracy | : Rule by old men |
| Gerontology | : Scientifics study of old age and process of ageing |

37. Gyn : **Female**

Gynaecology	: Science dealing with women's aliments
Misogynist	: One who hates women
Gynaecologist	: Doctor who treats women's diseases
Philogyny	: Fondness for women

38. Gene : **Origin**

Gene	: Unit of heredity in chromosome
Genesis	: Origin
Eugenics	: Science dealing with the improvement of the hereditary qualities of a race
Genetics	: Study of heredity and variation in organisms
Genealogy	: Pedigree
Congenital	: Existing from birth

39. -gamy, -gamo   : Marriage

Bigamy	: Crime of going through form of marriage while previous marriage is still in existence
Misogamist	: One who hates marriage
Monogamy	: Practice of being married to one person at a time
Polygamy	: A custom of having more than one wife

40. Geo   : From earth

Geography	: The science of the earth's surface
Geology	: The science of the earth's history

Geophysics	: Study of earth's magnetism
Geopolitics	: Country's politics as determined by its geographical position
Geocentric	: Representing the earth as centre

41. Hemi   **: Half**

Hemisphere	: Half of the globe
Hemialgia	: Pain on one side of the head
Hemihedron	: A crystal having half the usual number of faces

42. Hydro, Hydra   **: Water, moisture**

Hydraulics	: Use of water to drive machinery
Hydrotherapy	: Treatment of disease by the use of water
Hydrophobia	: Morbid fear of water
Hydrosphere	: The water vapour in the atmosphere
Hydroplane	: A sea plane
Hydroscope	: A device that enables you to see through great depths to the sea bed
Hydrostatics	: The principle of static applied to water

43. Hetero   **: Different**

Heterogeneous   Diverse in character; composed of diverse elements

Heterogamy   : Sexual reproduction involving fusion of unlike gametes

Heterocyclic   : Composed of atoms of more than one kind

Heteromorphic   : Occurring in two or more different forms

Heterochromatic   : Having different colours

44. Hyper   **: More**

Hyperthermia   : Very high body temperature

Hypermetropia   : Abnormal condition in which vision for distant objects is better than for near objects.

Hypertrophy   : Enlargement (of organ etc.)

Hyperinflation   : Rapid inflation

Hypertension   : Abnormally high blood pressure

Hypersonic   : Of or being a speed over five times that of the speed of sound (Mach 5)

Hyperphysical   : Supernatural

| Hyperbole | : Exaggerated statement |

45. Hypo : **Low or below**

Hypogeum	: Underground chamber
Hypogeal	: Existing or growing underground
Hypothermia	: Abnormally low body temperature
Hypodermic	: Of the parts beneath the skin
Hypotension	: Abnormally low blood pressure
Hypoplasia	: Arrested development in which an organ remains below the normal size

46. Inter : **Between, among, located between, carried on between**

Intermission	: An intervening period of time between acts of a performance
Intermittent	: Pausing or stopping at intervals
Intermediate	: Occurring at or near the middle place
Intermolecular	: Existing between molecules
Intermingle	: Mix together

47. -ine : **Of, Made up of**

Vulpine	: Like a fox
Leonine	: Like a lion
Lupine	: Like a wolf
Bovine	: Like a cow
Ursine	: Like a bear
Serpentine	: Like a snake
Feline	: Like a cat
Elephantine	: Of the nature of an elephant
Equine	: Like a horse
Divine	: Of the nature of God
Hircine	: Like a goat
Psittacine	: Of parrots, parrot-like
48. Intra	**: Within, inside, inward**
Intracranial	: Within the skull
Intracellular	: Functioning within a cell
Intramural	: Within the limits of community or institutions
Intrauterine	: Occurring inside the uterus

| Intravenous | : Within a vein |

49. –ic | **: Nature of, like**

Metallic	: Like a metal
Acidic	: Like an acid
Galactic	: Relating to the galaxy
Semitic	: Relating to Semites

50. –logy | **: Character of speech or language, subject of study, discourse**

Aetiology	: Science of the causes of disease
Archaeology	: Study of human antiquities
Aerology	: Study of atmosphere away from ground
Anthropology	: Study of mankind
Agrostology	: The branch of botany concerned with grasses
Aerobiology	: Study of air-borne micro organism
Amphibiology	: Branch of zoology treating of Amphibia
Balneology	: Scientific study of bathing and medicinal springs

Biology	: Science of life
Bacteriology	: Study of Bacteria
Bryology	: Study of mosses
Cardiology	: Study of the heart
Campanology	: Study of bells
Characterology	: Science of the development and variation of character
Chronology	: Science of computing dates
Conchology	: Study of shells and shellfish
Criminology	: Scientific study of crime
Codicology	: Study of manuscripts
Cosmology	: Science of the universe
Dendrology	: Study of trees
Deltiology	: Hobby of collecting postcards
Dermatology	: Study of skin and its diseases
Ecclesiology	: The study of church architecture and ornament
Ecology	: Study of interaction of persons with their environment

Enology	: The science of wine and wine making
Enzymology	: Science that deals with enzymes, their nature, activity and significance
Etymology	: The history of the origin and development of a word or other linguistic forms
Exobiology	: The branch of biology that deals with the search for extraterrestrial life and the effects of extraterrestrial surroundings on living organisms.
Entomology	: Study of insects
Egyptology	: Study of Egyptian antiquities
Eschatology	: Branch of theology concerned with the ultimate destiny of the universe or mankind
Ethnology	: Science that deals with the various forms of social relationships
Ethnomusicology	: The study of the music of non-European cultures
Ethology	: The study of the formation and evolution of human characters and beliefs
Etiology	: The study of the causes of origin, specifically of a disease or abnormal condition

Electrobiology   : Science of the electrical phenomena
                            of living beings

Epidemiology   : Science of epidemics

Graphology   : Study of character from handwriting

Glaciology   : Science of geological action of ice

Gynaecology   : Scientific study of women's ailments

Gerontology   : Scientific study of old age and
                            process of aging

Geomorphology   : Study of the physical features of the
                            earth's surface and their relation to its
                            geological structures

Geology   : Study of the earth

Haplology   : Mistake of uttering once what should
                            be spoken twice

Herpetology   : Study of reptiles

Heortology   : Study of religious festivals

Haematology   : Study of physiology of blood

Histology   : Study of organic tissues

Histopathology   : Study of changes in tissues caused
                            by disease

Hydrology	: Study of the movement, distribution, and quality of water on Earth and other planets
Hypnology	: Science of the phenomena of sleep
Indology	: Study of Indian history, literature etc.
Ichthyology	: Study of fishes
Iconology	: Study of icons
Kallology	: Study of beauty
Lithology	: Science of the nature and composition of rocks and stones
Malacology	: Science of molluscs or mollusks
Meteorology	: Study of motions and phenomena of atmosphere
Metrology	: Science or system of weights and measures
Morphology	: Study of the forms of things
Mineralogy	: Science of Minerals
Muscology	: Study of mosses
Musicology	: Study of the history, theory and physics of music

Mythology	: Study of myths
Neonatology	: Study of organisms not yet extinct
Nephology	: Study of the clouds
Nosology	: Branch of medical science dealing with classification of diseases
Numerology	: Study of occult meaning of numbers
Ontology	: Branch of metaphysics dealing with the nature of being
Ophthalmology	: Scientific study of the eye
Orology	: Study of mountains
Otology	: The branch of medicine that deals with the structure, function, and pathology of the ear
Ornithology	: Study of birds
Palaeography	: Study of ancient writings and inscriptions
Paleontology	: Study of life in the geological past
Palynology	: Study of pollen in connection with plant geography
Papyrology	: The study of papyrus manuscripts
Parapsychology	: Study of mental phenomena outside

the sphere of ordinary psychology

Pedology	: Science of natural soils
Pathology	: Science of bodily diseases
Patrology	: Study of writings of the fathers of the church
Penology	: Study of punishment of crime and of prison management
Periodontology	: Study of structures surrounding and supporting teeth
Petrology	: Study of origin, structure etc. of rocks
Pharmacology	: Science of action of drugs on the body
Phenology	: The scientific study of periodic biological phenomena, such as flowering, breeding, and migration, in relation to climatic conditions
Phenomenology	: Science of phenomena
Philology	: Science of languages
Phonology	: The study of speech sounds in language or a language with reference to their distribution and patterning and to tacit rules governing pronunciation.

Phraseology	: Study of set or fixed expressions, such as idioms, phrasal verbs, and other types of multi-word lexical units
Physiology	: Science of functions and phenomena of living organism and their parts
Rheumatology	: Study of rheumatic diseases
Rheology	: Science dealing with flow and deformation of matter
Radiology	: Scientific study of X-ray and other high-energy radiation
Synecology	: The study of the ecological interrelationships among communities of organisms
Stomatology	: Science of the mount
Splenology	: The branch of science which treats of the spleen
Speleology	: Scientific study of caves
Speciology	: Science of species
Somatology	: Science of living bodies physically concerned
Sociology	: Study of the nature and development of human society

Sinology	: Study of Chinese language, history, customs etc
Serology	: Scientific study of plasma serum and other bodily fluids
Semiology	: Branch of linguistics concerned with signs and symbols
Selenology	: Science of the moon
Seismology	: Study of earthquakes
Trilogy	: Group of three related literacy or operatic works
Toxicology	: Study of poisons
Topology	: Study of geometrical properties and spatial relations
Thermatology	: The study of heat as a medical remedy or therapy
Theology	: Study of religion
Terotechnology	: Branch of technology dealing with installation and maintenance of equipment
Terminology	: Science of proper use of terms
Teratology	: Study of animal or vegetable monstrosities

Technology	: Science of practical or industrial arts
Tribology	: Science of interacting surfaces in relative motion
Tautology	: Saying of the same things twice over in different words
Typology	: Study and interpretation of types
Vexillology	: Study of flags
Virology	: Scientific study of viruses
Volcanology	: Scientific study of volcanoes
Zoology	: Science of animal life

51. Mega : **Big or large**

Megalomania	: Delusions of bigness or grandeur
Megalith	: Big stone monument
Megaphone	: A device for magnifying sound
Megascopic	: Enlarged
Megadynamics	: Mechanics of major earth movement
Megalopolis	: A very large city
Megameter	: Instrument for observing the stars in order to determine longitude

52. Mater : **Pertaining to mother, female**

Matricide : The act of killing one's mother

Matron : A woman who acts as a supervisor or monitor in a public institution, such as a school, hospital, or prison.

Matriarchy : System of social organization in which the female is head of the family

Matrilocal : Of system of marriage where husband goes to live with wife's group

Maternity : Motherhood

Matriarch : A woman who rules a family, group or state

Matrimony : The act or state of being married; marriage

Matrilineal

: Of or tracing descent through the maternal line

53. Mal : **Bad, Wrongful, ill**

Maladjusted : Poorly adjusted

Malediction : A magical word or phrase uttered with the intention of bringing about evil or destruction; a curse

Malabsorption : Defective or inadequate absorption of nutrients from the intestinal tract

Malpractice	: An instance of improper conduct
Maladroit	: Showing or characterized by clumsiness; not dexterous
Malodorous	: Smelling very unpleasant or bad odor
Malcontent	: A person who is dissatisfied and rebellious
Malefactor	: One that has committed a crime; a criminal
Malnutrition	: Faulty or inadequate nutrition
Malversation	: Corruption in office

54. -mania : **Obsession, Craziness**

Monomania	: An unreasonable interest in one particular thing
Bibliomania	: Craze for collecting books
Egomania	: Morbid egotism →Morbid - unhealthy interest or diseased
Dipsomania	: Morbid craving for alcoholic liquor
Kleptomania	: A morbid impulse for stealing
Pyromania	: A morbid impulse to set fire
Erotomania	: Morbid sexual passion

Megalomania	: Delusion that one is great or powerful
Nymphomania	: Morbid sexual desire in women
Anglo mania	: Craze for what is English

55. Micro : Small

Microgram	: One million of a gram
Micromelia	: The condition in which a limb is abnormally shortened. *Also called nanomelia*
Microscope	: Instrument to examine small objects
Microcosm	: A small world
Microbe	: A small germ
Microphone	: An instrument for converting sound waves into electrical energy variations, which may then be amplified, transmitted, or recorded
Micrometer	: Instrument for measuring minute distances

56. Mono : One or single

| Monocracy | : Government by one person only |
| Monotone | : A succession of speech sounds in |

one unvarying pitch

Monolith	: Single block of stone esp. shaped into pillar or monument
Monandry	: Custom of having only one husband at a time
Monolingual	: Knowing or using only one language
Monocarpic	: Bearing fruit only once
Monarchy	: A state ruled or headed by a monarch
Monad	: A unit, one
Monoglot	: A person who knows only one language
Monocle	: Single eyeglass
Monologue	: Dramatic or literary soliloquy
Monorail	: Track consisting of a single rail
Monotheism	: Doctrine or belief that there is only one God
Monatomic	: Consisting of one atom
Monogyny	: Custom of having only one wife at a time
Monocephalus	: A malformed fetus with two bodies

and one head

57. Nat : **To be born**

Prenatal : Pertaining to the time before birth

Native : A person or animal born in one place

58. Neo : **New**

Neophyte : A new convert

Neology : The use of new words in language

Neoblastic : Having the nature of new growth

Neocracy : Government by new, inexperienced officials

Neonate : New born child

Neolatry : The worship of the new or novelty

Neogenesis : A new formation or regeneration of tissue

59. Octo : **Eight**

Octopod : An octopus with eight arms

Octavo : The page size, from 5 by 8 inches to 6 by 9 1/2 inches, of a book composed of printer's sheets folded into eight leaves. or A book composed of octavo pages.

Octave	: A group of 8 lines of a verse or a tone on the eighth degree from a given musical tone
Octogenarian	: A person between 80 and 89
Octoroon	: A person whose ancestry is one-eighth Black
Octagon	: A polygon of eight sides and eight angles
Octameter	: A line of verse consisting of eight feet
Octahedron	: A polyhedron of eight faces
Octad	: A series of eight or a group or set of eight
60. Oculo	**: Eye**
Ocular	: Of the eye, sight, visual
Oculist	: One who specialises in treatment of eye disorders
61. Omnis	**: All**
Omnific	: All-creating
Omnibus	: Serving several purposes at once
Omnidirectional	: Receiving or transmitting in all directions

Omnigenous	: Consisting of all kinds
Omnivorous	: Feeding on many kind of food
Omnicompetent	: Having jurisdiction in all cases, able to deal with all matters
Omnipotent	: Having infinite power
Omniscient	: All-knowing
Omnipresent	: Present everywhere
Omnifarious	: Comprising or relating to all sorts or varieties
Omnibus	: 1. A long motor vehicle for passengers; a bus. 2. A printed anthology of the works of one author or of writings on related subjects.

62. Ophthalmos : **Of the eye**

Exophthalmos	: Abnormal protrusion of the eyeball
Ophthalmology	: Scientific study of the eye
Ophthalmia	: Inflammation of the eye, specially conjunctivitis

63. Over : **Upper, higher**

| Overwhelm | : To cover over completely |

Overawe	: To fill with excessive fear
Overbuild	: To build in excess of demand
Overbearing	: Harshly masterful or domineering
Over strung	: Highly strung
Overbook	: To issue bookings in excess of space available
Overact	: Act (a role) in an exaggerated manner
Overate	: Overeat
Overbid	: Bid that is higher than another
Overblown	: Excessively inflated or pretentious
Overburden	: Burden (a person, thing, etc) to excess

64. -osis **: Action, process, Change**

Hypnosis	: A condition that resembles sleep
Metamorphosis	: Change of form
Thrombosis	: A condition resulting from the clotting of blood
Leukocytosis	: A condition due to excess of white cells

65. -phobia **: fear**

Anglophobia	: Fear of everything English
Aquaphobia	: Fear of water
Acrophobia	: Fear of heights
Astraphobia	: Fear of lightning and thunder
Agoraphobia	: Fear of open space
Algophobia	: Excessive fear of pain
Anthophobia	: Fear of flowers
Ailurophobia	: Fear of cats
Bacteriophobia	: Fear of bacteria, germs and microbes
Brontophobia	: Fear of thunder and thunderstorms
Clinophobia	: Fear of going to bed
Claustrophobia	: Fear of closed place
Cynophobia	: Fear of dogs
Dromophobia	: Fear of crossing roads
Demonophobia	: Fear of spirits and demons
Equinophobia	: Fear of horses
Gallophobia	: Fear of everything French

Hydrophobia   : Fear of water

Mysophobia   : Fear of dirt, germs, contamination

Nyctophobia   : Fear of night and darkness

Necrophobia   : Fear of dead bodies

Numerophobia   : Fear of number or numbers

Ophidiophobia   : Fear of snakes

Ochlophobia   : Fear of crowds

Pyrophobia   : Fear of fire

Phobophobia   : Fear of fear

Phonophobia   : Fear of speaking aloud

Photophobia   : Fear of light

Russophobia   : Fear of Russians and things Russian

Sitophobia   : Morbid aversion to food

Thalassophobia   : Fear of seas

Thanatophobia   : Fear of death

Xenophobia   : Fear of strangers

Zoophobia   : Fear of animals

66. Pre   **: Before**

Precaution	: Care taken before hand
Predict	: Foretell
Premonition	: A forewarning
Precocious	: Having ripened very early
Preamble	: An introduction
Presume	: To take to oneself a right before it has been granted

67. Post : After, Behind

Postmortem	: 1. Occurring or done after death. 2. Of or relating to a medical examination of a dead body.
Postscript	: Additional paragraph at the end of a letter
Postprandial	: After dinner
Postmeridian	: After the sun has passed the dividing line at noon

68. Ped : Foot

Pedestrian	: Going or performed on foot
Pedal	: Foot lever
Pedate	: Footed

Pedometer	: Instrument that records the distance a walker covers
Pedlar	: Travelling vendor of small wares
Pedicel	: A plant stalk that supports a fruit
Pedicure	: Treatment for the care of the feet and to nails
Podiatry	: Care and treatment of the human foot

69. Pseudo : **False**

Pseudologist	: One who utters falsehoods; a liar
Pseudosmia	: False sense of smell
Pseudoscience	: Science that is not true
Pseudodox	: A false opinion
Pseudonym	: A false name
Pseudopsia	: Visual hallucinations, illusions, or false perceptions
Pseudograph	: A false writing; a spurious document; a forgery
Pseudology	: A lie or Falsehood of speech
Pseudomania	: A mania for making false statements

70. Patho, Pathos, Pathy   **: Suffering**

Pathos

: A quality, as of an experience or a work of art that arouses feelings of pity, sympathy, tenderness, or sorrow.

Pathognomy

: Study of the emotions

Pathogen

: Agent causing disease

Pathology

: Science of bodily diseases

Sympathy

: Tendency to favour or support, expression of pity

Allopathy

: Treatment of disease by inducing an opposite condition

Empathy

: The capacity for participation in another's feelings or ideas

Pathetic fallacy

: The attribution of human characteristics or feelings to inanimate nature

Pathogenesis

: The origination and development of a disease

Pathetic

: Exciting pity

71. Pan   **: All**

Panacea

: A cure for all ill

Pantheon	: A temple dedicated to all Gods
Pantisocracy	: A community, social group, etc., in which all have rule and everyone is equal
Pandemic	: Relating all people, universal
Pansophy	: Universal wisdom
Panhuman	: Relating to all humanity

72. Paidos : Child

Paediatrics	: Relating to children and their diseases
Paedo-baptism	: Infant baptism

73. Psyche : Mind

Psyche	: The soul, self, mind
Psychiatry	: Branch of medicine that deals with mental, emotional or behavioural disorders
Psychic	: Originating in the mind, lying outside the sphere of physical science or knowledge
Psychogenic	: Originating in the mind or in mental or emotional conflict

Psychodynamic   : Science of the mental powers

Psychopath   : Person suffering from chronic mental disorder

Psychoneurosis   : A neurosis based on emotional conflict

Psychosurgery   : Brain surgery used to treat mental disorders

Psychotropic   : A psychotropic drug or other agent

Psychopathology   : The study of Psychological and behavioural aberrations in mental disorder

Psychoactive   : Affecting the mind

Psychosomatic   : Diseases caused or aggravated by mental stress

Psychosocial   : Relation of social conditions to mental health

74. Peri   **: Round, about**

Pericycle   : A thin layer that surrounds the central vascular part of many stems and roots

Pericardium   : The membrane that surrounds the heart of the vertebrates

Perimeter   : The boundary of a closed plane

| | figure |
| Perianth | : The external envelops of a flower |

75. Per   **: Through**

Perennial	: Through the years
Perforated	: Bored through
Perambulate	: To walk up and down
Peregrinate	: To walk through
Percolate	: To drip through

76. Poly   **: Many**

Polytheism	: Belief in many Gods
Polyphone	: A style of musical composition in which many related voice parts sound against one another
Polyandry	: Having more than one husband
Polylingual	: Containing matter in several languages
Polytechnic	: An institution devoted to many applied arts and sciences

77. Para   **: Besides, like**

| Parallel | : Extending alongside |

Parataxis	: The placing of clauses side by side
Paratyphoid	: A disease that resembles typhoid
Parable	: A story which teaches alongside a moral

78. Pater : **Father**

Paternal	: Fatherly
Patriarch	: Father and ruler of family or tribe
Patrilocal	: Of system of marriage where wife goes to life with husband's group
Patrilineal	: Relating to, based on, or tracing ancestral descent through the paternal line
Patrician	: Somebody of high birth
Patrimony	: Property inherited from one's father or ancestors, heritage
Paternity	: Fatherhood

79. –rupt : **To break**

Corrupt	: To destroy morally
Disrupt	: To break apart, throw into disorder
Interrupt	: To break into the continuity of

something such as conversion

Erupt   : To out burst forth with lava, steam
                         etc.

80. Re   **: Back, again**

Refund   : Pay back

Revise   : To read again

Recall   : To call back

Rebuff   : To reject or refuse abruptly or
                         rudely, snub

Rescind   : To take back

Recalcitrant   : Obstinately defying or resisting a
                         request or command

Reprieve   : To delay the execution of a sentence

81. Sub   **: Under, Beneath**

Subconscious   : Under the conscious level of the
                         mind

Subvert   : To undertake

Submerge   : To plunge under

Subscribe   : To underwrite, sign one's name
                         under a contract or letter

Subaltern	: Under another, inferior in rank
Subterraneous	: Underground
Subterfuge	: Deception, underhand method
Subterranean	: Operating under the surface of the earth
Subcutaneous	: Under the skin
Subfluvial	: Placed under a river, as a tunnel
Submission	: The act of putting oneself under the control of another

82. Senex **: Old**

Senescent	: Growing old
Senior	: Older, superior in age or standing to
Senile	: Showing the feebleness etc., of old age

83. Spect **: Watch, See**

Spectre	: A ghost
Spectrum	: Wavelengths of colour from red to violet
Spectacle	: A show
Spectrometry	: The measuring of wavelengths of

rays

Spectroscope : An instrument used to analyse spectra

Spectator : An observer

Spectrogram : A graphic or photographic representation of a spectrum

Spectrophobia : Fear of ghosts

Spectrohelioscope : An instrument for the observation of the sun

84. Syn : Together (with)

Syndrome : A set of symptoms that occur together

Synthesis : Bringing the separate parts together

Syndicate : An association of individuals coming to transact business

Syncopate : To shorten something by cutting part of it and piecing it together

Synchronize : To happen at the same time

Synagogue : A meeting place where Jews come together for worship

Synod : An assembly where people come together

85. Sur, Supra   **: Above**

Surpass   : Go beyond

Surreal   : Heaving a dreamlike irrational quality transcending reality

Surplus   : Excess

Surcoat   : Loose robe worn over armour

Surcharge   : Overload; to overprint, to subject to an additional charge

Supremacy   : Being supreme

Supramaxillary   : Of the upper jaw

Supramundane   : Above or superior to the world

Supranational   : Transcending national limits

86. –ship   **: status, period during which a position is held, state, condition, quality of, office**

Membership   : Forming part of a group

Friendship   : Being friends

Professorship   : Holding the position of a professor

Lordship   : Title for a lord, the authority of a lord

Readership	: The office, duties or position of a reader
Scholarship	: The character and attainments of a scholar
Dictatorship	: Being a dictator

87. Sangui : **Blood**

Sanguify	: Conversion of food into blood
Sanguine	: Red, like blood
Sanguinary	: Blood thirsty
Sang-froid	: Coolness, composure
Consanguinity	: Blood relationship
Sanguimotor	: Relating to the circulation of blood

88. –tude : **State**

Beatitude	: State of heavenly bliss
Fortitude	: Passive courage, resolute endurance
Solitude	: State of being alone
Attitude	: Manner, feeling toward
Solicitude	: State of concern for another
Turpitude	: Baseness, depravity

Rectitude	: State of righteousness
Pulchritude	: State of beauty, loveliness
Plenitude	: State of fullness
Vicissitude	: Changes especially with regard to the affairs of life of the world, an alternating state

89. Tri **: Three**

Treble	: Three times the number
Triangle	: A polygon of three sides and three angles
Tricycle	: A three wheeled vehicle
Triad	: A group of three people
Trichotomy	: Division into three parts
Triceps	: A muscle with three points of attachment
Trident	: Three pronged spear

90. Tele **: Long distance**

| Telex | : Communication service |
| Telecommunication | : Communication at a distance |

Telepathy	: Communication at a distance
Telemeter	: An apparatus for measuring a quantity and transmitting the result to a distant point
Telescope	: Instrument for viewing distant objects
Teleport	: To transport oneself from one place to another using only the power of one's mind
Telephotography	: The photography of distant objects

91. Uni **: One**

Unicorn	: A mythical animal with one horn
Unicellular	: Consisting of a single cell
Uniaxial	: Having only one axis
Unicameral	: Having a single legislative chamber
Unicycle	: Any vehicle with a single wheel
Unilateral	: One sided, performed by or affecting only one person or party

92. Ultima **: to come to an end, Last**

| Ultima | : Final |
| Ultimo | : Last month, the month preceding the |

present

Ultimatum	: The final offer
Ultima ratio	: The last and final argument
Ultima Thule	: The last inhabitable place
Ultimogeniture	: A law by which the youngest son, the last born, inherits the estate

Test Series

Test- 1

1. Give one word

1. Able to use left and right hands equally = _____________
2. Dislike or feeling of aversion = _____________
3. A chief angel = _____________
4. Study of Measurement of the human body = _____________
5. Cluster of stars = _____________
6. Medicine given to counteract poison = _____________
7. Lover of mankind = _____________
8. The act of pulling = _____________
9. One who hates mankind = _____________
10. Area in acres = _____________
11. To set free from control = _____________
12. To keep apart = _____________
13. To make sacred = _____________
14. Antiquated, utterly out of date = _____________
15. Consisting of two legislative chambers = _____________
16. The flora and fauna of a region = _____________
17. A blessing = _____________
18. Part of the world in which life exists = _____________
19. Able to speak two languages with ease = _____________
20. The act of being married a second time
while previous marriage is still = _____________

2. Choose the correct synonyms

1. Astronaut
 a) Space Traveller
 b) Study of Stars
 c) Excavate
 d) Origin

2. Emancipate
a) Head
b) To set free from control
c) Mode of life
d) To bring forth

3. Ambiguity
a) Active
b) Double meaning
c) Simplicity
d) Cunning

4. Anthropometry
a) Vegetable
b) Study of measurement of the human body
c) Zenith
d) Study of mankind

5. Antenatal
a) Immune
b) After birth
c) Before death
d) Occurring previous to birth

6. Antipathy
a) Lone
b) Sympathy

c) Aversion
d) Pain

7. Monarch
a) Rule by a father
b) Rule by a woman
c) Queen
d) The single or sole ruler of a state

8. Archetype
a) A Prototype
b) Old
c) Veteran
d) Rubbish

9. Haulage
a) Action
b) Antidote
c) The act of pulling
d) The act of drinking

10. Benediction
a) Blessings
b) Benefitted
c) Word to word
d) Cure

Test- 2

Give one word

1. The killing of race   = __________
2. A roundabout way of saving something   = __________
3. The killing of one's sister   = __________
4. The killing of one's mother   = __________
5. To order in opposition to an order
previously given thereby annulling it   = __________
6. The killing of one's wife   = __________
7. An undertaker   = __________
8. A doctor whose specialty is care of children   = __________
9. Articles brought into the country
against the law   = __________
10. A huge vessel for boiling   = __________
11. State of being static, motionless   = __________
12. A long and bitter discussion which
is usually abusive   = __________
13. Cut into, as incise an abscess or infection   = __________
14. Of or relating to the head   = __________
15. Mal development of reading ability
in otherwise normal children   = __________
16. State of unease or mental discomfort   = __________
17. The outer layer of an embryo at a
very early stage in its development   = __________
18. Surgical removal of the uterus   = __________
19. A leader who exploits the weaknesses
of the mob   = __________
20. One on whom a benefice is bestowed   = __________

2. Choose the correct synonyms

1. Biopsy
a) Examination
b) Living
c) Examination of living tissue
d) A drink

2. Bilingual
a) Man
b) South Indian
c) Able to speak two languages
d) Bad Man with ease

3. Genocide
a) Killing of Man
b) Killing of a race
c) Killing of insects
d) Killing of mother

4. Contravene
a) Come across
b) Conflict with
c) To get smaller
d) Lovable

5. Circumvent
a) To get around
b) Irreverent
c) Crooked
d) Long

6. Mortician
a) Car
b) An undertaker

c) Caretaker
d) Foreigner

7. Dysphoria
a) A blessing
b) State of Wellbeing
c) Mode of life
d) State of unease or mental discomfort

8. Diatribe
a) Lovable
b) Bitter discussion
c) Good natured
d) Sheer of Gauzy

9. Demagogue
a) Villain
b) Hero
c) Selfish
d) A misleading leader or teacher

10. Dormant
a) Sleeping
b) Active
c) Excellent
d) Foolish

Test - 3

1. Give one word

1. A state of equilibrium, a counter balance   =___________
2. Having all sides equal   =___________
3. Subject to two or more interpretations   =___________
4. Outermost layer of embryo in early development   =___________
5. Capable of development apart from the host   =___________
6. The practice of talking about oneself too much   =___________
7. One's other self   =___________
8. To dig out of ground   =___________
9. To breathe out   =___________
10. To come off in layers   =___________
11. One who hates women   =___________
12. Rule by old men   =___________
13. Having many bends   =___________
14. Bend the knee esp. in worship   =___________
15. Going straight to the point without ambiguity   =___________
16. Fondness for women   =___________
17. Pedigree   =___________
18. Science dealing with the improvement of the hereditary qualities of a race   =___________
19. One who hates marriage   =___________
20. A custom of having more than one wife   =___________

2. Choose the correct synonyms

1. Excision
a) Taking in
b) Removing off
c) Bringing
d) Get out

2. Ectozoan
a) Cut short
b) Personal
c) External parasite
d) Acting

3. Equipoise
a) Equally distant
b) Having Equal sides
c) Equal in force
d) A counter balance

4. Egoist
a) Intractable
b) Stubborn
c) Selfish person
d) Dead

5. Epigastric
a) Skin
b) Lying on or over the stomach
c) Upper part of head
d) Foot

6. Hysterectomy
a) Ulcer removal
b) A name of dog

c) Convulsions
d) Ancient

7. Egomania
a) Selfish
b) Morbid Egotism
c) Patriotic
d) Self-centered

8. Ecosystem
a) Economics
b) Science of sound
c) Ruling system
d) System for interacting organisms in a particular habitat

9. Exophthalmoses
a) Exhibition
b) Abnormal protrusion of the eyeball
c) Eyes
d) External eye ball

10. Exhume
a) To dig out
b) To dig in
c) Grow
d) Engrave

Test- 4

1. Give one word

1. Pain on one side of the head =__________
2. Fear of water =__________
3. A sea plane =__________
4. A device that enables you to see through great depths to the sea bed =__________
5. Sexual reproduction involving fusion of unlike gametes =__________
6. Having different colours =__________
7. Exaggerated statement =__________
8. Of or being a speed over five times that of the speed of sound =__________
9. Existing or growing underground =__________
10. Of the parts beneath the skin =__________
11. Arrested development in which an organ remains below the normal size =__________
12. Mix together =__________
13. Like a bear =__________
14. Like a fox =__________
15. Like a cow =__________
16. Of parrots, parrot-like =__________
17. Within a vein =__________
18. Within the skull =__________
19. Within the limits of community or institutions =__________
20. Relating to the galaxy =__________

2. Choose the correct synonyms

1. Fortress
a) Palace
b) A fortified place
c) A big house
d) A hut

2. Flection
a) Edible
b) Penny less
c) Happy
d) Curvature, Bend

3. Forthright
a) Correct
b) Going straight to the point
c) Precise
d) Ambiguity without ambiguity

4. Congenital
a) Flow
b) Existing from birth
c) Ancestral
d) From fore father

5. Gerontology
a) Study of words
b) Study of children
c) Study of old age
d) Study of birds

6. Geography
a) Digging earth
b) Knowing about maps

c) Travelling to new places
d) The science of the earth's surface

7. Polygamy
a) Simple
b) Sports
c) A synthetic cloth
d) A custom of having more than one wife

8. Misogynist
a) Unmarried
b) Female Doctor
c) Philanderer
d) One who hates women

9. Hypotension
a) Dampness
b) Low blood pressure
c) Excessive love
d) High blood pressure

10. Ambidextrous
a) Environment
b) Double meaning
c) Doubtfulness
d) Able to use both hand with equal ease

Test- 5

1. Give one word

1. Study of mankind   =__________
2. Study of mosses   =__________
3. Science of the causes of disease   =__________
4. Study of air-borne micro organism   =__________
5. Scientific study of bathing and medicinal
springs   =__________
6. Science of the universe   =__________
7. Study of trees   =__________
8. Study of bells   =__________
9. The study of church architecture and
ornament   =__________
10. The history of the origin and development
of a word or other linguistic forms   =__________
11. The study of the formation and evolution
of human characters and beliefs   =__________
12. The science of wine and wine making   =__________
13. Scientific study of old age and process
of aging   =__________
14. Science of geological action of ice   =__________
15. Study of reptiles   =__________
16. Study of beauty   =__________
17. Study of fishes   =__________
18. Study of the forms of things   =__________
19. Study of organisms not yet extinct   =__________
20. Study of mountains   =__________

2. Choose the correct synonyms

1. Hyperthermia
a) Temperature
b) Coldness
c) Anger
d) Very high temperature of body

2. Heterochromatic
a) Coloured glasses
b) Colour blindness
c) Having different colour
d) Mixture

3. Hydrophobia
a) Fear of love
b) Fear of water
c) Fear of strangers
d) Instrument of measuring water flow

4. Hemisphere
a) Globe
b) Sphere
c) A box
d) Half of the globe

5. Intermingle
a) Mix together
b) Get separated
c) Burst
d) Flexor

6. Divine
a) Villain
b) Recreant

c) Of the nature of God
d) Miscreant

7. Intrauterine
a) Internal
b) Getting along
c) Like a bull
d) Occurring inside the uterus

8. Mineralogy
a) Science of mines
b) Science of minerals
c) Science of Rocks
d) Science of own

9. Monoglot
a) Foolish
b) Poor
c) Person using one language
d) Ignoring

10. Megalith
a) A dress
b) Small monument
c) Imagine
d) Big stone monument

Test- 6

1. Give one word

1. Scientific study of the eye = _____________
2. Study of occult meaning of numbers = _____________
3. Study of writings of the fathers of the church = _____________
4. Study of rheumatic diseases = _____________
5. Science of species = _____________
6. Science of the mouth & its diseases = _____________
7. Study of earthquakes = _____________
8. Study of poisons = _____________
9. Scientific study of viruses = _____________
10. Instrument for observing the stars in order to determine longitude = _____________
11. Big stone monument = _____________
12. The act of killing one's mother = _____________
13. System of social organization in which the female is head of the family = _____________
14. Clumsy = _____________
15. Corruption in office = _____________
16. An unreasonable interest in one particular thing = _____________
17. A morbid impulse for stealing = _____________
18. Craze for what is English = _____________
19. Morbid craving for alcoholic liquor = _____________
20. A small world = _____________

2. Choose the correct synonyms

1. Matriarch
a) Mother
b) Motherly love
c) Curves
d) Rule by a woman

2. Malediction
a) Curse
b) A good saying
c) Revenge
d) Exhale

3. Microbe
a) A small germ
b) Economics
c) Instrument to see
d) Flat

4. Metamorphosis
a) Outgoing
b) Similarity
c) Change of form
d) Foolish

5. Neophyte
a) A new convert
b) Consummate
c) One who collects coins
d) Impost

6. Octopod
a) Extrovert
b) An octopus with eight arms

c) An insect
d) Chair

7. Ominous
a) Carriage
b) Serving several purposes at once
c) Electronic media
d) Technology

8. Ocular
a) Face
b) Of the eye, sight, visual
c) An instrument
d) Scientific

9. Overbuild
a) Changes
b) Multi storied building
c) Infrastructure
d) To build in excess of demand

10. Pathogen
a) Feelings
b) Agent causing disease
c) Backing
d) Origin

Test- 7

1. Give one word

1. Knowing or using only one language = _______________
2. Single block of stone especially shaped
into pillar or monument = _______________
3. A unit, one = _______________
4. Custom of having only one wife at a time = _______________
5. Pertaining to the time before birth = _______________
6. A new convert = _______________
7. Government by new, inexperienced officials = _______________
8. New born child = _______________
9. An octopus with eight arms = _______________
10. A polygon of eight sides and eight angles = _______________
11. One who specializes in treatment of
eye disorders = _______________
12. Serving several purposes at once = _______________
13. Having infinite power = _______________
14. Present everywhere = _______________
15. Scientific study of the eye = _______________
16. To fill with excessive fear = _______________
17. Inflated or pretentious = _______________
18. A condition resulting from the
clotting of blood = _______________
19. A condition due to excess of white cells = _______________
20. Fear of heights = _______________

2. Choose the correct synonyms

1. Predict
a) Foretell
b) Introduction
c) Downfall
d) After death

2. Polygamy
a) Simple
b) Sports
c) A synthetic cloth
d) A custom of having more than one wife

3. Pedestrian
a) Child specialist
b) A walker
c) Horse rider
d) Sick

4. Pseudonym
a) Nemesis
b) Hybrid
c) A false name
d) Longing

5. Psychoactive
a) Mad
b) Never disease
c) Affecting
d) Emotional

6. Polylingual
a) God of Hindus
b) Different caste

c) Grand parents
d) Containing matter in several languages

7. Percolate
a) To drip through
b) To see
c) To act
d) Squeezing

8. Panacea
a) Cure for all
b) Greek God
c) Hall of fame
d) A leaf of chew

9. Perimeter
a) Come together
b) All around
c) The boundary of close
d) Instrument to measure distance figure

10. Postmortem
a) After death
b) Possessive
c) Living tissue
d) Dead body

Test- 8

1. Give one word

1. Excessive fear of pain = __________
2. Fear of closed place = __________
3. Fear of snakes = __________
4. Fear of water = __________
5. Fear of dirt, germs, contamination = __________
6. Fear of dead bodies = __________
7. Fear of fire = __________
8. Fear of crowds = __________
9. Fear of strangers = __________
10. Fear of animals = __________
11. A forewarning = __________
12. After the sun has passed the dividing line at noon = __________
13. Going or performed on foot = __________
14. Treatment for the care of the feet and to nails = __________
15. A mania for making false statements = __________
16. A false name = __________
17. The capacity for participation in another's feelings or ideas = __________
18. A cure for all ill = __________
19. Relating to all humanity = __________
20. Infant baptism = __________

2. Choose the correct synonyms

1. Parataxis
a) Corruption
b) Impulse
c) The placing of clauses
d) Concern side by side

2. Paternity
a) Fatherhood
b) Motherhood
c) Brotherhood
d) Sisterhood

3. Erupt
a) Snake
b) Burst of lava
c) Volcano
d) Corrupt

4. Reprieve
a) Go away
b) To prove
c) To delay the execution
d) Deceived of a sentence

5. Sanguify
a) Sing
b) Conversion of food into blood
c) Relation
d) Brother

6. Senile
a) Talkative
b) Child

c) Child

d) Showing the feebleness of old age

7. Subvert

a) To undermine

b) To come forward

c) Deceive

d) Drown

8. Supremacy

a) Beauty Queen

b) Clean

c) Being supreme

d) Dashing

9. Specter

a) Police

b) Ghost

c) To visualize

d) Fairy

10. Syndrome

a) Similar

b) A set of symptoms that

c) Sleepy

d) Musical instrument occur together

Test- 9

1. Give one word

1. Of drug acting on the mind =______________
2. The membrane that surrounds the
heart of the vertebrates =______________
3. The external envelops of a flower =______________
4. To drip through =______________
5. Belief in many Gods =______________
6. A story which teaches alongside a moral =______________
7. Father and ruler of family or tribe =______________
8. Somebody of high birth =______________
9. To reject or refuse abruptly or rudely, snub =______________
10. To take back =______________
11. Deception, underhand method =______________
12. Placed under a river, as a tunnel =______________
13. The act of putting oneself under the
control of another =______________
14. Showing the feebleness etc., of old age =______________
15. An instrument used to analyse spectra =______________
16. An instrument for the observation
of the sun =______________
17. A meeting place where Jews come
together for worship =______________
18. An assembly where people come together =______________
19. Loose robe worn over armour =______________
20. Above or superior to the world =______________

2. Choose the correct synonyms

1. Synchronous
a) Similar
b) Different
c) Happening at precisely
d) With place the same time

2. Lordship
a) Title for a lord
b) Courtship
c) Benevolent
d) The authority of a lord

3. Plentitude or Plenitude
a) Fresh
b) State of fullness
c) Cushioned
d) Dig out

4. Trident
a) Shrill voice
b) Three pronged spear
c) Sweet voice
d) Accident

5. Telepathy
a) Sympathy
b) Communication from one mind to another
c) Love
d) Own thinking mind to another

6. Ultima
a) Initial
b) A spice

c) Final
d) A name

7. Uniaxial
a) Unit
b) Singular
c) Having only one axis
d) Proceed

8. Unicorn
a) A mythical horse like animal with a single horn
b) Having or consisting of a single cell
c) Having a single legislative chamber
d) Unbroken

9. Spectroscope
a) Like prism
b) An optical instrument used for forming spectra for study
c) Colour Spectrum
d) Wavelength measuring instrument

10. Spectroscopy
a) A speculum
b) Muse, reflect
c) The study of spectra by use of the spectroscope
d) Cogitate

Answer Key

Test-1

Answers

1. Give one word	2. Choose the correct synonyms
1. Ambidextrous	1. a
2. Antipathy	2. b
3. Archangel	3. b
4. Anthropometry	4. b
5. Asterism	5. d
6. Antidote	6. c
7. Philanthropist	7. d
8. Haulage	8. a
9. Misanthrope	9. c
10. Acreage	10. a
11. Emancipate	
12. Segregate	
13. Consecrate	
14. Antediluvian	
15. Bicameral	
16. Biota	
17. Benediction	
18. Biosphere	
19. Bilingual	
20. Bigamy	

Test-2

Answers

1. Give one word	2. Choose the correct synonyms
1. Genocide	1. c
2. Circumlocution	2. c
3. Sororicide	3. b
4. Matricide	4. b
5. Countermand	5. a
6. Uxoricide	6. b
7. Mortician	7. d
8. Pediatrician	8. b
9. Contraband	9. d
10. Cauldron	10. a
11. Dormancy	
12. Diatribe	
13. Incise	
14. Cephalic	
15. Dyslexia	
16. Dysphoria	
17. Epiblast	
18. Hysterectomy	
19. Demagogue	
20. Collate	

Test- 3

Answers

1. Give one word	2. Choose the correct synonyms
1. Equipoise	1. b
2. Equilateral	2. c
3. Equivocal	3. d
4. Ectoderm	4. c
5. Ectogenous	5. b
6. Egotism	6. a
7. Alter ego	7. b
8. Exhume	8. d
9. Exhale	9. b
10. Exfoliate	10. a
11. Misogynist	
12. Gerontocracy	
13. Flexuous	
14. Genuflect	
15. Forthright	
16. Philogyny	
17. Genealogy	
18. Eugenics	
19. Misogamist	
20. Polygamy	

Test - 4

Answers

1. Give one word	2. Choose the correct synonyms
1. Hemialgia	1. b
2. Hydrophobia	2. d
3. Hydroplane	3. b
4. Hydroscope	4. b
5. Heterogamy	5. c
6. Heterochromatic	6. d
7. Hyperbole	7. d
8. Hypersonic	8. d
9. Hypogeal	9. b
10. Hypodermic	10. d
11. Hypoplasia	
12. Intermingle	
13. Ursine	
14. Vulpine	
15. Bovine	
16. Psittacine	
17. Intravenous	
18. Intracranial	
19. Intramural	
20. Galactic	

Test - 5

Answers

1. Give one word	2. Choose the correct synonyms
1. Anthropology	1. d
2. Bryology	2. c
3. Aetiology or etiology	3. b
4. Aerobiology	4. d
5. Balneology	5. a
6. Cosmology	6. c
7. Dendrology	7. d
8. Campanology	8. b
9. Ecclesiology	9. c
10. Etymology	10. d
11. Ethology	
12. Enology	
13. Gerontology	
14. Glaciology	
15. Herpetology	
16. Kallology	
17. Ichthyology	
18. Morphology	
19. Neonatology	
20. Orology	

Test - 6

Answers

1. Give one word	2. Choose the correct synonyms
1. Ophthalmology	1. d
2. Numerology	2. a
3. Patrology	3. a
4. Rheumatology	4. c
5. Speciology	5. a
6. Stomatology	6. b
7. Seismology	7. b
8. Toxicology	8. b
9. Virology	9. d
10. Megameter	10. b
11. Megalith	
12. Matricide	
13. Matriarchy	
14. Maladroit	
15. Malversation	
16. Monomania	
17. Kleptomania	
18. Anglo mania	
19. Dipsomania	
20. Microcosm	

Test - 7

Answers

1. Give one word	2. Choose the correct synonyms
1.Monolingual	1. a
2.Monolith	2. d
3.Monad	3. b
4.Monogyny	4. c
5.Prenatal	5. c
6.Neophyte	6. d
7.Neocracy	7. b
8.Neonate	8. a
9.Octopod	9. c
10.Octagon	10. a
11.Oculist	
12.Omnibus	
13.Omnipotent	
14.Omnipresent	
15.Ophthalmology	
16.Overawe	
17.Overblown	
18.Thrombosis	
19.Leucocytosis	
20.Acrophobia	

Test - 8

Answers

1. Give one word	2. Choose the correct synonyms
1. Algophobia	1. d
2. Claustrophobia	2. a
3. Ophidiophobia	3. b
4. Hydrophobia	4. c
5. Mysophobia	5. b
6. Necrophobia	6. d
7. Pyrophobia	7. a
8. Ochlophobia	8. c
9. Xenophobia	9. b
10. Zoophobia	10. b
11. Premonition	
12. Postmeridian	
13. Pedestrian	
14. Pedicure	
15. Pseudomania	
16. Pseudonym	
17. Empathy	
18. Panacea	
19. Panhuman	
20. Paedobaptism	

Test - 9

Answers

1. Give one word	2. Choose the correct synonyms
1.Psychotropic	1. d
2.Pericardium	2. a
3.Perianth	3. b
4.Percolate	4. b
5.Polytheism	5. b
6.Parable	6. c
7.Patriarch	7. c
8.Patrician	8. a
9.Rebuff	9. b
10.Rescind	10. c
11.Subterfuge	
12.Subfluvial	
13.Submission	
14.Senile	
15.Spectroscope	
16.Spectrohelioscope	
17.Synagogue	
18.Synod	
19.Surcoat	
20.Supramundane	

PART- 2

WORDS DENOTING

1. WORDS DENOTING PLACES

A place where fish are kept	: Aquarium
A place where rabbits are kept	: Hutch
A place where pigs are kept	: Sty
A place for keeping and breeding insects	: Insectarium
The house or shelter of an Eskimo	: Igloo
The house or shelter of a Swiss peasant	: Chalet
The house or shelter of an Arab	: Douar
The house or shelter of an American Indian	: Wigwam, tepee
A place where Government records are kept	: Archives
A place where manufacture is carried on	: Factory
A place where house refuse is reduces to ashes	: Incinerator
A place where athletic exercises are performed	: Gymnasium
A place or room for the collection of dried plants	: Herbarium

A place where treasures of art, curiosities, etc are preserved or exhibited	: Museum
A place where treasures, stores, ammunition are hidden	: Cache
A place for storing grain	: Granary
A place where goods are stored	: Depot
An upper room or storey immediately under the roof	: Garret
A place where leather is tanned	: Tannery
A building for the lodging and accommodation of soldiers	: Barracks
A place where milk is converted into butter and cheese	: Dairy
A place where animals are slaughtered for the market	: Abattoir
A place where spirituous liquors are produced	: Distillery
A place where clothes are washed and ironed	: Laundry
A place for housing cars	: Garage
A place for housing aero planes	: Hangar

A place where travellers may obtain lodging and refreshment	: Hotel, Inn
A place where people may obtain food and refreshment	: Restaurant
A variety show performed in a Restaurant	: Cabaret
The kitchen of a ship	: Caboose, Galley
A house for the residence of the students	: Hostel
A place where soldiers are quartered	: Cantonment
A place where money is coined	: Mint
A place where astronomical observations are taken	: Observatory
A place where fruit trees are grown	: Orchard

2. WORDS DENOTING MARRIAGE

To run away with a lover in order to get married secretly	: Elope
Proclamation of intended marriage	: Banns
A bride's outfit	: Trousseau
Engaged to be married	: Betrothed, Affianced
One engaged to be married	: Fiancé, Fiancée
The property which a new wife brings to her husband	: Dowry
A woman whose husband is dead	: Widow
A man whose wife is dead	: Widower
Payment of money allowed to a wife on legal separation from her husband	: Alimony
One who has only one wife or husband at a time	: Monogamist
One who marries a second wife or husband while the legal spouse is alive	: Bigamist
Man who has more than one wife at a time	: Polygynist
Woman who has more than one husband at a time	: Polyandrist

A hater of marriage	: Misogamist
One vowed to a single or unmarried life	: Celibate
Legal dissolution of the marriage of husband and wife	: Divorce

3. WORDS DENOTING DEATH

To dig up a corps	: Exhume
A frame on which a dead body is conveyed	: Bier
A pile of wood on which a dead body is burned	: Pyre
A vehicle for taking dead bodies to the cemetery	: Hearse
A place where dead bodies are interred	: Cemetery
An examination of a dead body	: Postmortem, Autopsy
Occurring after death	: Posthumous
An inscription on a tomb	: Epitaph
A vault beneath to church used for burial	: Crypt
A stone coffin, especially one made of limestone	: Sarcophagus
Underground caves with burying places for the dead	: Catacombs
A very expensive and elaborately built tomb	: Mausoleum
The practice of putting painlessly to	: Euthanasia

death	
An account in the newspaper of the funeral of one deceased	: Obituary
To die, without leaving a will	: Intestate
The property left to someone by a will	: Legacy
Mass for the dead	: Requiem
Killed by an electric current	: Electrocuted
A monument set up for persons who are buried elsewhere	: Cenotaph
Fainting on death due to being deprived of air	: Asphyxia
The dead body of a human being	: Corpse
The dead body of an animal	: Carcass
A place where dead bodies are temporarily placed	: Mortuary
A place where the bodies of persons found dead are placed for identification	: Morgue
Disposal of a dead body by burning	: Cremation
To preserve a dead body from putrefaction	: Embalm
The cloth which is wrapped round a	: Winding - sheet

dead body	

4. WORDS DENOTING NATURE STUDY

Living or operating equally on land and in water	: Amphibious
Living or going in flocks or herds	: Gregarious
The dormant condition in which plants and animals pass the winter	: Hibernation
(Trees) which lose their leaves annually	: Deciduous
A cud-chewing animal, e.g. the cow	: Ruminant
A gnawing animal	: Rodent
A four-footed animal	: Quadruped
Animals which carry their young in a pouch, e.g. kangaroo	: Marsupials
Soil composed largely of decayed vegetable matter	: Humus
Soil washed down and carried away by rivers	: Alluvium
A preparation for killing insects	: Insecticide
A plant or animal growing on another	: Parasite
The green colouring matter in the leaves of plants	: Chlorophyll
Tiny openings on the under-surface of	: Stomata

leaves through which the plant breathes	
The process by which plants take up mineral salts in solution through their roots	: Absorption
The process by means of which plants and animals breathe	: Respiration
The process by which plants manufactured food	: Assimilation
The process by which plants give off excess water through their leaves	: Transpiration
The process by which the young plant begins to grow	: Germination
The part of the embryo which forms the stem	: Plumule
The part of the embryo which forms the root	: Radicle
That part of the seed which develops into the plant	: Embryo, Germ
Living for many years	: Perennial
Lasting for two years	: Biennial
Lasting for a single year or season	: Annual
A plant or animal growing on another	: Parasite

A slimy substance between the wood and bark of a stem	: Cambium
Two leaf-life appendages at the base of some leaves	: Stipules
A spiral shoots of a plant which winds itself round another body for support	: Tendril
The process by which pollen dust is transferred from the stamen to the pistil	: Pollination
The entrance of the pollen grains into the ovules in the ovary	: Fertilisation
An instrument for making holes in the soil for seeds or seedlings	: Dibble
Animals with backbone	: Vertebrates
Animals without backbone	: Invertebrates
The inside of a nut	: Kernel
The central or innermost part of a fruit	: Core
The animals of a certain region	: Fauna
The plants and vegetation of a certain region	: Flora
The last stage through which an insect passes before it becomes a perfect	: Chrysalis

insects	
Absence of rain for a long time	: Drought
One who studies plant and animal life	: Naturalist
The parts of an animal killed for food which are rejected or considered waste	: Offal
Rock from which metal is extracted	: Ore
The track of a wild animal	: Spoor
The meat of deer	: Venison
The flesh of sheep	: Mutton
A cluster of flowers on a branch	: Inflorescence
The seed-leaves of the embryo	: Cotyledon
Plants with one seed-leaf, e.g. corn	: Monocotyledonous
Plants with two seed-leaves, e.g. lime	: Dicotyledonous
A thick underground stem	: Rhizome
The dead skin cast off by a snake	: Slough
The feelers of an insect	: Antennae
To supply land with water by artificial means	: Irrigate

5. WORDS DENOTING NEGATIVES

Incapable of making errors	: Indestructible
Incapable of being redeemed from evil i.e. beyond corrections	: Incorrigible
Incapable of being burn	: Incombustible
That which cannot be avoided or prevented	: Inevitable
That which cannot be made plain or understood	: Inexplicable
Enduring for all times	: Imperishable
Not admitting the passage or entrances of water etc	: Impervious
Not endowed with animal life	: Inanimate
Absolutely necessary cannot be dispensed with	: Indispensable
Not to the point	: Irrelevant
Unable to die	: Immortal
That which cannot be moved	: Immovable
That which cannot be heard	: Inaudible
That which cannot be seen	: Invisible

That which cannot be pierced or penetrated	: Impenetrable
That which cannot be taken by assault	: Impregnable
That which cannot be passed	: Impassable
That which cannot be conquered	: Invincible
That which cannot be wounded or injured	: Invulnerable
That which cannot be lessened	: Irreducible
That which cannot be repaired or remedied	: Irreparable
That which cannot be made good in case of loss	: Irreplaceable
That which cannot be imitated	: Inimitable
That which cannot be rubbed out or blotted out	: Ineffaceable, Indelible

6. WORDS DENOTING SCIENTIFIC INSTRUMENTS

An instrument which when put to both eyes enables a person to see distant objects as if they were near	: Binoculars
An instrument used for measuring heat or cold	: Thermometer
An instrument for measuring the pressure of air	: Barometer
An instrument for measuring the force or variation of the wind	: Anemometer
An instrument for measuring electric current	: Ammeter
An instrument for recording revolutions	: Gyrograph
An instrument for making very small objects appear large	: Microscope
An instrument for distinguishing precious stones	: Lithoscope
An instrument for transmitting the voice to a distance	: Telephone
An instrument for measuring gases	: Manometer
An instrument for increasing the volume of the voice	: Microphone
An instrument for enabling persons	: Periscope

inside a submarine to see objects above the surface of the water	
An instrument for detecting earthquakes	: Seismograph
An instrument for taking photographs	: Camera
An instrument for measuring the speed of a motor-car	: Speedometer
An instrument for beating time during a musical performance	: Metronome
An instrument for measuring minute distances	: Micrometer
A hydrometer for determining the specific gravity, and richness of milk	: Lactometer

7. WORDS DENOTING MILITARY WORDS

A number of ships travelling together under escort for the sake of safety	: Convey
Smuggling of goods or engaging in prohibited traffic	: Contraband
An unprovoked attack by an enemy	: Aggression
Nations carrying on warfare	: Belligerents
Compulsory enrolment as soldiers or sailors	: Conscriptions
The killed or wounded in battle	: Casualties
To make an examination or preliminary survey of enemy territory or military objective	: Reconnoitre
A number of firearms being discharged continuously	: Fusillade
Foot-soldiers	: Infantry
Horse-soldiers	: Cavalry
The firing of many guns at the same time to mark an occasion	: Salvo
The act or practice of spying	: Espionage
To remove from one place to another to avoid the destruction of war	: Evacuate

An order prohibiting ships to leave the ports	: Embargo
To make troops, ships etc ready for war service	: Mobilise
Taking neither side in the struggle, that is, not assisting either of the belligerents	: Neutral
To enter a country as an enemy	: Invade
A shower of bullets	: Volley
An apparatus which opens like an umbrella to enable a person to drop safely from an aircraft	: Parachute
A place where naval or military weapons are made or stored	: Arsenal
A foreigner in a belligerent country	: Alien
To keep citizens in confinement	: Intern
Shells, bombs, military stores	: Ammunition
Heavy guns, artillery and army stores	: Bayonet
A promise given by a prisoner not to try to escape if given temporary release	: Parole
Long strips of cloth bound round the legs of a soldier from the ankle to the	: Puttees

knee	
A place where naval or military weapons are made or stored	: Arsenal
Music for awakening soldiers in the morning	: Reveille
A place where soldiers can buy drinks and other refreshments	: Canteen
An agreement to stop fighting	: Armistice
To surrender to any enemy on agreed terms	: Capitulate
To camp in the open air without tents or covering	: Bivouac
An encampment in the open air	: Bivouac
To release from the army	: Demobilise
To reduce to nothing	: Annihilate
A general pardon of offenders	: Amnesty
The main division of army	: Battalion
To seize for military use	: Commandeer
Movement of ships or troops in order to secure an advantage over the enemy	: Manoeuvre
To surround a place with the intention	: Besiege

of capturing it	
A soldier recently enlistee for service	: Recruits
A soldier's holiday	: Leave, Furlough
Official reports on the progress of the war	: Bulletin
The art of conducting negotiations between nations	: Diplomacy
A body of soldiers stationed in a fortress to defend it	: Garrison
A board belt worn across the shoulder and chest, with pockets for carrying ammunition	: Bandolier
A person who is forced by law to become a soldier	: Conscript
An irregular warfare conducted by scattered or independent bands	: Guerrilla war
Movement of ships or troop in order to secure an advantage over the enemy	: Manoeuvre

8. WORDS DENOTING LITERARY

A book of accounts showing debits and credits	: Ledger
A book in which the events of each day are recorded	: Diary
A book of names and address	: Directory
A book containing the words of a language with their definitions, in alphabetical order	: Dictionary
A book containing information on all branches of knowledge	: Encyclopaedia
An error or misprint in printing, or writing	: Erratum
An exact copy of handwriting, printing or a picture	: Facsimile
A principle or standard by which anything is, or can be judged	: Criterion
Delivered (of a speech) without previous preparation	: Extempore, Impromptu
A short speech by a player at the beginning of a play	: Prologue
A book with blank pages for putting pictures, autographs, stamps, etc	: Album

A list of books in a library	: Catalogue, Bibliography
A list of explanation of rare, technical or obsolete words	: Glossary
A written account, usually in book form, of the interesting and memorable experiences of one's life	: Memoirs
The trade mark of the maker seen on paper when it is held up to the light	: Watermark
One who pretends to have a great deal of knowledge	: Wiseacre
The exclusive right of an author or his heirs to publish sells copies of his writings	: Copyright
A picture facing the title of a book	: Frontispiece
A brief summary of a book	: Epitome
An extract or selection from a book of writing	: Excerpt
The heading of short description of a newspaper article, chapter of a book etc.	: Caption
A statement which is accepted as true without proof	: Axiom
A list of the headings of the business to	: Agenda

be transacted at a meeting	
Language which is confused and unintelligible	: Jargon
A declaration of plans and promises put forward by a candidate for election, a political party or a sovereign	: Manifesto
To remove the offensive portions of a book	: Expurgate
Still in use (of books published long ago)	: Extant
A succession of the same initial letters in passage	: Alliteration
A note to help the money	: Memorandum
A list of articles and their description	: Inventory
The concluding part of a speech	: Peroration
A noisy of vehement speech intended to excite passions	: Harangue
To make expressive gestures or motions while speaking	: Gesticulate
Language that is very much used	: Hackneyed
To pronounce words distinctly	: Enunciate
One who writes plays	: Dramatist,

	Playwright
A poem in which the first letters of each line, taken in order, form a name or a sentence	: Acrostic
A short speech by a player at the end of a play	: Epilogue
Passing off another author's work as one's own	: Plagiarism
A writing or speech in praise of a person	: Eulogy, Encomium
A person's own handwriting	: Autograph
A record of one's life written by himself	: Autobiography
The history of the life of a person	: Biography
A humorous play, having a happy ending	: Comedy
A play with a sad or tragic end	: Tragedy
A mournful song (or poem) for the dead	: Dirge
A conversation between two persons	: Dialogue
Speaking to oneself	: Soliloquy
Study by night	: Locum

9. ONE WORD FOR A PHRASE OR A CLAUSE

A person who hates marriage	: Misogamist
At the point of the death	: Moribund
A contemptible term for a school master	: Pedagogue
A style in which the writer tries to show off his learning	: Pedantic
A person indifferent to pleasure or pain	: Stoic
One who walks in sleep	: Somnambulist
One who talks in sleep	: Somniloquist
A homeless and helpless person, esp. a neglected or abandoned child	: Waif
A building where dead body are kept	: Mortuary, Morgue
A lightweight umbrella carried by women	:Parasol
A person who is fond of fighting	: Bellicose
To renounce the crown in favour of someone	: Aborigines
The school, college, or university that one once attended. Or The anthem of a school, college, or university.	: Alma Mater

That which is inherited from the forefathers	: Ancestral
The secret art of transmuting base metals into gold	: Alchemy
A thing which is easily broken	: Brittle
An insect with many legs	: Centipede
A man whose manners are most like those of a woman than a man	: Effeminate
Exalted state of feeling especially of joy	: Ecstasy
One who leaves his native place to settle in another	: Emigrant
One who comes to a foreign land to settle here	: Immigrant
A person who dies without making his will	: Intestate
To give one's authority to another	: Delegate
Allowance due to a wife from husband consequent upon separation	: Alimony
One who cannot be corrected	: Incorrigible
Men living in the same age or period	: Contemporaries
An office or post with salary but no work	: Sinecure

Speech made to oneself when left alone	: Soliloquy
One who abstains from drinking	: Teetotaller
A specialist in care for the feet	: Podiatrist
A breaker of images in religious worship	: Iconoclast
One who is gradually recovering his health	: Convalescent
Words inscribed on the tomb of a person	: Epitaph
A book giving knowledge on all branches of knowledge	: Encyclopaedia
Hastily erected barrier across the street	: Barricade
The worship of sacred images	: Iconolatry
Narrow neck of land connecting two bigger land masses	: Isthmus
Violation of what is sacred	: Sacrilege
A room for practice of physical exercises	: Gymnasium
An unexpected piece of good fortune	: Windfall
An entertainer who performs gymnastic feats	: Acrobat

An official pardon for people who have been convicted of political offenses.	: Amnesty
Liable to be easily made angry	: Irritable
A person who does not believe in God	: Atheist
A person who is exceedingly greedy	: Avaricious
One who is not professional	: Amateur
One who has given up religion	: Apostate, Renegade
The branch of acoustics concerned with speech processes including its production and perception and acoustic analysis	: Phonetics
On speaking many languages	: Linguist
Animals living in flocks	: Gregarious
Dull uniformity	: Monotony
Fertile place with water and trees, in desert of the earliest found in a country at the time	: Aborigines
A disease that spreads by contact or touch	: Contagious
In capable of being seized	: Elusive

A man who eats human flesh	: Cannibal
Animals which live in water	: Aquatic
A person who believes in or advocates anarchism	: Anarchist
A collection of small choice poems	: Anthology
A partner in a crime	: Accomplice
A person who holds that nothing is known or likely to be known of the existence of God	: Agnostic
A masculine woman	: Amazon
A person who can use both hands with the same skills	: Ambidextrous
A statement which is obscure or capable of more than one interpretation	: Ambiguous
One who can be easily duped	: Fatalist
One who is not easily pleased by anything	: Fastidious
To attack or injure the reputation by slanderous statements	: Defame
An extemporaneous speech or remark	: Impromptu
An extremely lazy person	: Indolent

One who is unable to pay one's debts	: Insolvent
A rising up against established authority	: Insurrection
That which cannot be overcome	: Insurmountable
A wrong use of a word	: Misnomer
Sole right to make and sell some invention	: Patent
Person who is made to bear the blame due to others	: Scapegoat
An unmarried woman	: Spinster
Child who stays away from school without leave	: Truant
A number of stars grouped together	: Constellation
A large body of water with many islands	: Ocean
A person fond of refined sensuous enjoyments	: Epicure
Favoritism of relatives in bestowing offices	: Nepotism
Mental weariness from lack of occupation	: Ennui
To be reserved in speech	: Reticent

| Tendency to fight | : Pugnacity |
| Wrongful entry into another person's house or land | : Trespass |

10. WORDS DENOTING NUMBERS

A number of sheep	: Flock
A number of whales	: School
A large number of fish swimming together	: Shoal
A number of fish taken in a net	: Catch
A number of birds, e.g. partridge	: Convey
A number of asses	: Pack
A number of horses, ponies, etc. driven together	: Drove
A number of cattle are swine feeding or driven together	: Herd
A number of oxen or horses (two or more) harnessed together	: Team
A number of birds, bees or insects moving together	: Flight
A number of peacocks	: Muster
A number of wolves, hounds or submarines	: Pack
A number of leopards	: Leap
A number of geese	: Gaggle

A number of bees, locusts, ants etc	: Swarm
A number of larks or quails or beautiful girls	: Bevy
A number of bees living in the same place	: Hive
A number of ants, rabbits or snakes living in the same place	: Nest
A number of horses kept for riding, racing and breeding	: Stud
A number of lions, monkeys or cavalry soldiers	: Troop
A number of rooks	: Rookery
A colony of seals	: Rookery
A number of mules	: Barren
A number of chickens hatched at the same time	: Brood
A number of young pigs, dogs, cats brought forth at one birth	: Litter
A number of kittens	: Kindle
A collection of fowls, ducks etc	: Poultry
A couple of hawks	: Cast

A number of wild geese or swans in flight	: Skein
A collection of wild animals	: Menagerie, Zoo
A number of people at church	: Congregation
A number of people listening to a concert or lecture	: Audience
A number of people looking on at a football match etc	: Spectators
A number of people collected together in the street	: Crowd
A number of people gathered together for some common purpose	: Gathering, Assembly
A group of people who get together to work for some cause or common interest	: Coterie
A number of disorderly people	: Mob, Rabble
A number of savages	: Horde
A number of singers in a church	: Choir
A collection of angels	: Host
A number of artistes, dancers or acrobats	: Troupe

A number of actors	: Company
A number of servants	: Staff
A number of persons, of the same race, character, etc	: Tribe
A number of people following a funeral	: Cortege
A number of beautiful ladies	: Bevy
A number of soldiers	: Army, Regiment
A number of sailors	: Crew
A number of workmen, prisoners, thieves, etc	: Gang
A collection of slaves	: Gang, Coffle
A group of constables called to enforce the law	: Posse
A number of jurymen engaged on a case	: Jury, Panel
A number (more than two) of judges or bishops	: Bench
A number of directors of a company	: Board
A collection of poems	: Anthology
A collection of books	: Library

A number of pictures, curiosities, etc	: Collection
A collection of pearls	: Rope
A collection of flowers	:Bouquet
A collection of flags	: Bunting
A number of drawers	: Chest
A number of ships	: Fleet
A number of merchant ships protected by warships	: Convoy
A collection of dried plants	: Herbarium
A set of bells placed together for a tune to be played on them	: Carillon
A collection of tools	: Set
A bundle of hay	: Truss
A number of hired applauders i.e. persons paid to clap	: Claque
A mass of hair	: Shock, Fell
A quantity of bread baked at the same time	: Batch
A quantity of thread or yarn wound in a coil	: Skein

A collection of eggs	: Clutch
A collection of rays	: Pencil
A number of stars grouped together	: Constellation
A cluster of houses in a village	: Hamlet
A collection of wood, hay, corn, piled together	: Stack
A large collection of trees	: Forest
A number of nuts, grapes on a bunch	: Cluster

11. WORDS DENOTING PROFESSIONS OR TRADES

One who attends to the diseases of the eye	: Oculist
One who tests eyesight and sells spectacles	: Optician
One who attends to sick people and prescribes medicines	: Physician
One who compounds or sells drugs	: Druggist, pharmacist
One who treats diseases by performing operations	: Surgeon
A person whose profession is the care of teeth	: Dentist
A specialist in care for the feet	: Chiropodist
One physician who assists women at child-birth	: Obstetrician
One who treats diseases by rubbing the muscles	: Masseur
One who drives a motor-car	: Chauffeur
One who manages or attends to an engine	: Engineer
The naval officer in command of a military ship	: Captain

The commander of a fleet	: Admiral
One who carves in stone	: Sculptor
One who cuts precious stones	: Lapidary, lapidist
One who writes for the newspapers	: Journalist, reporter, correspondent
One who sets type for books, newspapers etc	: Compositor
One who plans and draws the design of buildings and superintends their erection	: Architect
One who draws plans	: Draughtsman
One who converts raw hide into leather	: Tanner
One who makes or deals in cutting instruments, e.g. knives	: Cutler
One who cleans the street	: Scavenger
A woman employed to clean inside building	: Charwoman
One who sells sweets and pastries	: Confectioner
A person in charge of a museum	: Curator

One who travels from place to place selling religious articles	: Colporteur
One who mends shoes	: Shoemaker, cobble
One employed as a labourer to do excavating work	: Navy
One who makes and sells ladies hats	: Milliner
One who sells small articles such as ribbons, laces, thread	: Haberdasher
One who deals in cloths and other fabrics	: Draper
A dealer in textiles (especially silks)	: Mercer
A professional rider in horse races	: Jockey
One who shoes horses	: Ferrier
One who pays out money at a bank	: Cashier, teller
One who lends money at exorbitant interest	: Usurer
One who draws maps	: Cartographer
One who collects postage stamps	: Philatelist
One who performs tricks by sleight of hand	: Conjurer, prestidigitator, Juggler

One who walks on ropes	: Funambulist
One who performs daring gymnastic feats	: Acrobat
One who pastures cattle for the market	: Grassier
An official in a hospital who looks after the social and material needs of the patients	: Almoner
The person incharge of a library	: Librarian
The head of a college	: Principal
The head of town council or corporation	: Mayor
One who lends money and keeps goods as security	: Pawnbroker
One who draws up contracts and also lends money on interest	: Scrivener
One who builds ships	: Shipwright
One who loads and unloads ships	: Stevedore
One versed in the science of human races, their varieties and origin	: Ethnologies
One who makes or sells candles	: Chandler
One who works or deals in feathers for	: Plumassier

apparel

The treasurer of a college or university	: Bursar
An officer in charge of the stores provisions and accounts on a ship	: Purser
One who makes wheels for carriages and carts	: Wheelwright
One who sells articles at public sells	: Auctioneer
A tradesman who manages funerals	: Undertaker
One skilled in the treatment of disease of animals	: Veterinarian
One who writes shorthand	: Stenographer
One who writes poetry	: Poet
One who write novels	: Novelist
One who write books	: Author
One who compiles dictionary	: Lexicographer
One who sells paper, ink, pens and writing materials	: Stationer
One who preserves the skins of animals and mounts them so as to resemble the living animals	: Taxidermist

12. WORDS DENOTING CHARACTERS

A lover of animals	: Zoophiles
One new to anything	: Novice, Tyro, Neophyte
A soldier or a sailor newly enlisted	: Recruit
One who is compelled by law to serve as a soldier	: Conscript
One who offers his service of his own free will	: Volunteer
One who retires from society to live a solitary life	: Recluse, Hermit
One who dies for a noble cause	: Martyr
One who breaks images or church ornaments	: Iconoclast
One who steals books	: Biblioklept
One who has an irresistible tendency to steals	: Kleptomaniac
One who maliciously sets fire to a building	: Incendiary
One who looks on the bright side of things	: Optimist
One who looks on the dark side of	: Pessimist

things	
One who devotes his service or wealth for the love of mankind	: Philanthropist
A hater of mankind	: Misanthrope, Misanthropist
One who becomes the favourite of distinguished personage and serves him as a slave	: Minion
One who sneers at the aims and beliefs of his fellow men	: Cynic
Someone who walks about in their sleep	: Somnambulist
Someone who talks while asleep	: Somniloquist
One who has the art of speaking in such a way that the sound seems to come from another person	: Ventriloquist
A conceited and self-centred person	: Egotist
One who devotes his life to the welfare and interest of other people	: Altruist
One who runs away from justice or the law	: Fugitive
One who takes refuge in a foreign country	: Refugee, Alien

A person who is expelled from home or country by authority	: Exile
One who engages in any pursuit for the love of it, and not for gain	: Amateur
One who feeds on fruits	: Fruitarian
One who eats no animal flesh	: Vegetarian
One who feeds on human flesh	: Cannibal
One who journeys from place to place	: Itinerant
One who journeys on foot	: Pedestrian
One who journeys to a holy place	: Pilgrim
One who goes from place to place begging alms	: Mendicant
One who can use both hands	: Ambidextrous
One versed in many languages	: Linguist
One who can enable people speaking different languages to understand each other	: Interpreter
One who imitates the voice, gesture etc. of another	: Mimic
One who pretends to know a great deal about everything	: Mountebank, Charlatan, Quack

One who pretends to be what he is not	: Hypocrite, Impostor
One given to sensual pleasures and bodily enjoyment	: Voluptuary
A leader of the people who can sway his followers by his oratory	: Demagogue
A person who reasons with clever but fallacious arguments	: Sophist
One who makes a display of his learning	: Pedant
One who has special skill in judging art, music, tastes, etc	: Connoisseur
An expert at story-telling	: Raconteur
One who listens to the conversation of others	: Eavesdropper
One who loves his country and serves it devotedly	: Patriot
One who foretells events	: Prophet
One devoted to the pleasures of eating and drinking	: Epicure
One given up to luxurious living	: Sybarite
One who kills political figures	: Assassin

A partner in crime	: Accomplice
One who works along with another	: Coadjutor
One living at the same time as another	: Contemporary
One who is opposed to intellectual progress	: Obscurant
One who eats all kinds of food	: Pantophagist
One who has an irresistible desire for alcoholic drinks	: Dipsomaniac, Alcoholic
One who abstains from alcoholic drinks	: Teetotaller
A person who invites guests to a social event (such as a party in his or her own home) and who is responsible for them while they are there	: Host, Hostess
One who accompanies a young lady to public places	: Chaperon
One under the protection of another	: Protege, Ward
One who searches for minerals or mining sites	: Prospector
A messenger sent in great haste	: Courier
One who steers a boat	: Coxswain
An acrobat who bends his body into	: Contortionist

various shapes	
A hater of marriage	: Misogamist
One who takes over after another in office or employment	: Successor
A person who precedes or preceded another, as in office	: Predecessor
One who collects coins	: Numismatics
A person who collects things belonging to ancient times	: Antiquary
An unthankful person	: Ingrate
a specialist in correcting deformities of the skeletal system (especially in children)	: Orthopedist
One who tries to get votes for an election candidate	: Canvasser
One who worries a candidate for election by interruption and awkward questions	: Heckler
A person in a low state of health or over-anxious about his health	: Valetudinarian
A hater of women	: Misogynist
A woman with light coloured hair	: Blonde

A woman with dark hair	: Brunette
A person who dresses up women's hair	: Hairdresser, Coiffeur
A noisy, abusive, scolding woman	: Termagant
A young lady who is making her first appearance at a public dance or being presented at court	: Debutante
One who hides away on a ship to obtain a free passage	: Stowaway
One who shoots with bows and arrows	: Archer
One who fishes with a rod	: Angler

13. WORDS DENOTING GOVERNMENTS

Government of the people for the people and by the people	: Democracy
Government by a sovereign with uncontrolled authority	: Autocracy, Despotism
Government by the nobility	: Aristocracy
Government by departments of state	: Bureaucracy
Government by a few	: Oligarchy
Government by the wealthy	: Plutocracy
Government by priests or ecclesiastics	: Hierarchy
Government by divine guidance	: Theocracy
The period between two reigns	: Interregnum
To decide a political question by the direct vote of the whole electorate	: Referendum
A radical change in government	: Revolution
The science of government	: Politics
The right of self-government	: Autonomy
Government by the worst citizens	: Aristocracy
Government by a military class	: Stratocracy

Government of a church by bishops	: Episcopacy
Facts and figures	: Statistics
An official numbering of the population	: Census
The wife or husband of a king or queen	: Consort
One who governs a kingdom during the infancy, absence or disability of the sovereign	: Regent

14. WORDS DENOTING CHURCH

The district under the jurisdiction of a bishop	: Diocese
The principal church in the diocese	: Cathedral
A passage between the pews in a church	: Aisle
One who has charge of a church building	: Sexton
One who leads people to their seats in a church	: Verger
The money given by the congregation at a church service	: Offertory
The ceremony at which a man becomes a priest	: Ordination
A bishop's staff	: Crosier
A bishop's cap	: Mitre
The garments of parsons and choristers	: Vestments
A long loose gown worn by priests and choristers	: Cassock
A loose white vestment worn over the cassock	: Surplice
A vestment like a surplice worn by	: Richet

bishops	
A cloak-like vestment worn by priests at processions or solemn ceremonies	: Cope
A chapel or vault beneath a church in which vestments are kept and in which church officials meet	: Vestry
The residence of a priest or minister or vicar	: Presbytery, Vicarage
One who sings in the choir	: Chorister
A reading-desk from which the scriptures are read	: Lectern
The stand from which a preacher delivers his sermon	: Pulpit
A breaker of church images or ornaments	: Iconoclast
The central or main part of a church	: Nave
The eastern end of a church	: Chancel
A portion of a large church or public institution set apart with an alter of its own where services can be held for a small number of people	: Chapel
One who assists at services by lighting candles etc	: Acolyte

A vessel for burning incense	: Censer
The salary of a clergyman	: Stipend
Method of administering Holy Communion by dipping the bread into the wine and offering both at once	: Intinction
The land furnishing part of the church revenue	: Glebe
One who renounces his religious vows or for sakes his religious Principles	: Apostate
One who is converted to one religion to another	: Proselyte
One who believes in single God	: Monotheist
One who believes in many Gods	: Polytheist
One intolerantly devoted to a particular creed	: Bigot
To utter profane language against God or anything holy	: Blaspheme
Holding opinions contrary to the true doctrine of the church so as to cause of a division	: Heresy
Violating or profaning religious things	: Sacrilege
The cup used in the Eucharist	: Chalice

The priest officiating at the Holy communion	: Celebrant
A rich covering carried over a priest in procession	: Canopy
The body of ministers ordained for the work in the Christian church	: Clergy
The people at distinct from the clergy	: Laity
A council of clergymen	: Synod
The vessel of basin containing water for baptism	: Font
The head of a cathedral	: Dean
A clergyman next in rank after a bishop	: Archdeacon
One in the lowest degree of holy orders in the Anglican church	: Deacon
A clergyman assigned to a regiment, a warship, prison or public Institution	: Chaplain
The circle of light seen in pictures around the head of Jesus Christ, the Virgin Mary, and the Saints	: Halo, Aureole
One who goes to heathen countries to spread the Gospel of Christ	: Missionary
Morning service of the Anglican Church	: Matins

Evening service	: Vespers
One who does not believe in the existence of God	: Atheist
One who believes that can have no knowledge of God but only of natural phenomena	: Agnostic

15. Animals and their gender

Animal	Male	Female
Antelope	Buck	Doe
Hare	Buck	Doe
Ass	Jackass	Jenny ass
Hartebeest	Bull	Cow
Badger	Boar	Sow
Horse	Stallion	Mare
Bear	Boar	Sow
Impala	Ram	Ewe
Bobcat	Tom	Lioness
Jackrabbit	Buck	Doe
Buffalo	Bull	Cow
Kangaroo	Buck	Doe
Camel	Bull	Cow
Leopard	Leopard	Leopardess
Caribou	Stag	Doe
Lion	Lion	Lioness

Cat	Tom	Queen
Moose	Bull	Cow
Cattle	Bull	Cow
Ox	Bullock	Cow
Chicken	Cock	Hen
Peacock	Peacock	Peahen
Cougar	Tom	Lioness
Pheasant	Cock	Hen
Coyote	Dog	Bitch
Pig	Boar	Sow
Deer	Stag	Doe
Rhinoceros	Bull	Cow
Dog	Dog	Bitch
Roe deer	Roebuck	Doe deer
Donkey	Jackass	Jenny ass
Seal	Bull	Cow
Duck	Drake	Duck

Sheep	Ram	Ewe
Eland	Bull	Cow
Swan	Cob	Pen
Elephant	Bull	Cow
Tiger	Tiger	Tigress
Ferret	Jack	Jill
Walrus	Bull	Cow
Fish	Cock	Hen
Weasel	Boar	Cow
Fox	Fox	Vixen
Whale	Bull	Cow
Giraffe	Bull	Cow
Wolf	Dog	Bitch
Goat	Billy goat	Nanny goat
Zebra	Stallion	Mare
Goose	Gander	Goose

16. Animal and their young

Animal	Young
Antelope	Kid
Ox	Stote
Badger	Cub
Pig	Piglet
Bear	Cub
Roe deer	Kid
Bobcat	Kitten
Sheep	Lamb
Camel	Calf
Swan	Cygnet
Chicken	Chick
Toad	Tadpole
Coyote	Puppy
Weasel	Kit
Dog	Puppy
Wolf	Cub

Eland	Calf
Elk	Calf
Beaver	Kitten
Frog	Tadpole
Buffalo	Calf
Giraffe	Calf
Caribou	Fawn
Goose	Gosling
Cougar	Kitten
Hartebeest	Calf
Deer	Fawn
Horse	Foal
Duck	Duckling
Kangaroo	Joey
Elephant	Calf
Lion	Cub
Fish	Fry

Goat	Kid
Fax	Cub
Hare	Leveret
Rhinoceros	Calf
Hawk	Chick
Seal	Calf
Jackrabbit	Kitten
Skunk	Kitten
Leopard	Cub
Tiger	Cub
Monkey	Infant
Walrus	Cub
Pheasant	Chick
Whale	Calf
Zebra	Foal

17. Collective terms

Animal	Collective
Antelope	Herd
Dog	Pack
Ape	Shrewdness
Donkey	Drove
Ass	Drove
Duck	Paddling
Badger	Cete
Eland	Herd
Bear	Sleuth
Elephant	Herd
Beaver	Colony
Elk	Gang
Bloodhound	Sute
Ferret	Business, cast, fesnying
Boar	Sounder
Fish	School

Buffalo	Herd
Fox	Troop
Camel	Train
Gelding	Brace
Caribou	Herd
Giraffe	Herd
Cat	Cluster
Goat	Flock
Cattle	Herd
Goose	Gaggle
Chamois	Herd
Hare	Husk
Chicken	Flock
Hartebeest	Herd
Chough	Chattering
Hawk	Cast
Colt	Rag

Horse	Herd
Coot	Fleet
Impale	Couple
Coyote	Pack
Jackrabbit	Husk
Deer	Herd
Kangaroo	Troop

18. Words expressing the cries of various animal and birds

Animal/birds	Cries
Apes	Gibber
Flies	Buzz
Asses	Bray
Frogs	Croak
Bears	Growl
Goats	Bleat
Beetles	Drone
Hens	Cackle, cluck
Bulls	Bellow
Jackals	Howl
Cats	Mew, purr
Lambs	Bleat
Cock	Crow
Lions	Roar
Crows	Caw

Monkeys	Chatter, gibber
Doves	Coo
Owls	Hoot, screech
Eagles	Scream
Pigeons	Coo
Puppies	Yelp
Elephants	Trumpet
Rooks	Caw
Foxes	Yelp, bark
Sheep	Bleat
Geese	Cackle
Squirrels	Squeak
Hawks	Scream
Swans	Cry
Horses	Neigh
Tigers	Roar
Kittens	Mew
Vultures	Scream

Larks	Sing
Wolves	Howl
Mice	Squeak
Bees	Hum
Nightingales	Sing, warble
Birds	Sing, chirp, twitter
Parrots	Talk
Camels	Grunt
Pig	Grunt, squeal
Cattle	Low
Ravens	Croak
Cows	Low
Serpents	Hiss
Dogs	Bark, yelp, howl
Sparrows	Chirp, twitter
Ducks	Quack
Swallows	Twitter

Thrushes	Whistle

19. Homes of persons, animals and birds

Persons/animals/birds	Home
Convict	Prison
Fowl	Coop
King	Palace
Horse	Stable
Lunatic	Asylum
Lion	Den
Monk	Monastery
Mouse	Hole
Nun	Convent
Owl	Barn or tree
Soldier	Barracks
Pigeon	Dove-cote
Bee	Hive
Rabbit	Burrow
Bird	Nest
Sheep	Pen or fold

Cow	Byre
Spider	Web
Dog	Kennel
Tiger	Lair

9 788819 075131 5